Synoptical Firing of Electrical Complexity

EVAN AMRHEIN

outskirts press

Outskirts Press, Inc.
http://www.outskirtspress.com

ISBN: 978-1-4787-9767-8

PRINTED IN THE UNITED STATES OF AMERICA

ELECTRICAL COMPLEXITY

This book is dedicated to my sister, Kristen Amrhein, the writer of the family. Only after she went home at the young age of eighteen did I have any interest of writing. The gift she left me. With out her constant involvement, my insight on life would not be as great as it is.

Pondering perspectives of reality

Contents

Here we go

1
GRATITUDE

Driven By Failure
5-2-96

Driven by failure and criticism
I must succeed
That's my creed
That's my goal
No more stress
A millionaire to be
You'll see
Here today
Here tomorrow
Here to stay
And that's okay
I'm sound
Something to see
Full of energy
Positively, someone to follow
If you can keep up
On top of the world today
On top of the world in everyway
Stretching through everyday
Here I am
Watch me go and grow

Aspersion
3-25-98

Opinionated Insinuating
God-Damn aspersion
Nothing but false opine contamination
Plagued with bacteria
Deserved ophthalmic gouging
Evaporated in a flash
Systematic evolution
Religious revolution
Can't sleep
Thinking to deep
Need an alteration of the mind
To calm my hideously snarling nerves
Emancipate
Emaciate
Emasculate
It's all good
Or is it?

My Piquant Angel

10 21-09

She's my piquant angel
She's magical
She's mystical
She's mysterious
She's my piquant angel
Beautiful
Beautiful
Beautiful
She's so beautiful
She was sent from heaven
To make my life better
To add happiness
Clarity....laughter....meaning
She's my piquant angel
Glowing with reason
Beaming with brilliance
She's remarkable
She's spectacular
Irresistible
Kind hearted
She's my piquant angel

I Love My Baby
6-10-09

I love my baby
I love my baby
I love my baby
She makes me real
She makes me feel
I get butterflies
When I see her
All the time
All the time
All the time
I love her dearly
She makes me laugh
From the stomach
From the stomach
From the stomach
So beautiful
So beautiful
I love my baby
I love my baby
I love my baby
Beautiful in everyway
Tender
Gentle
Exceptional
The best part
She's mine
All mine
So beautiful
So beautiful

So kind
So kind
So sweet
So sweet
I am so glad we met
I love my baby

Love
9-07-91

Your smile is enhancing
Your beauty is entrancing
Ever lasting
I miss you so much
Always thinking of you
I want to be with you
I want to feel you
I miss all the fun we
Have had
All of the laughter
We have shared together
All of the love
We have shown each other
I have yet to meet anyone as special as you
Anyone as exuberant as you
Anyone as exquisite as you
You are very beautiful to me
Not only as a person but
As a companion as well
In waking every morning
I know where ever I go
Someone loves me
As much as
I love them

I Know You Are Near
9-17-01

I can hear your voice
I can see your shadow
And I know you are near
I can feel your Presence
Smell your essence
An incredible ebullience of happiness
Has over taken my body
And my mind
You are not only my special love
But my special friend as well
I love you so much
You are far from being egregious
Instead, you are a very astonishingly
Sensational person
Beautiful on the inside
As well as the out side

Your eyes
9-6-91

Your eyes
Your provocative eyes
Relaying unspoken messages of
Passion, of love, of power
Looking into your eyes
I am in entranced by your beauty
By your charm
Your overpowering seductiveness
I am under your spell
Hypnotized by my elusive
Compulsiveness for you
You have touched me in a way
No one has ever before
I am addicted to you
I can’t stop thinking of you
Dreaming of you
Loving you
You are very dear to me
I desire you quit a lot
I have succumbed to
Your provocative eyes

My Beautiful Everything
1-2-98

My beautiful everything
So elegant
So unique
My beautiful everything
So special
So precious
Prettier than any bouquet
More beautiful than
The most colorful rainbow
Glowing with absolute kindness
So radiant with care
Your tenderness and sincerity
Fills me with extreme bliss
I am so happy
I have met you
Lucky I am
When I look into the sky
And the clouds part
Exposing sun rays
That beam down from the heavens above
I think how beautiful
And I think of you
How lucky I am to have met you
I love you with all my heart
With all my soul
I am going to love you
Until the day I die
My beautiful everything

Imprintation
9-6-16

Expectations caused by centrifugal
Explosions of assimilated
Complexity, materialized by
An infusion of intro-gated
Grid like patterns
Subconsciously imprinted over
Long periods of time
Causing your mind to think
And act accordingly to
Preconceived notions
Materialized by an
Atmospheric indulgence of
A consumed absorption
Of pervious executions

She's An Angel
11-20-09

She's an angel
I tell you
She's incredible
I tell you
She's extraordinary
I tell you
She's so beautiful
I tell you
I love her so much
I love her so much
She's beautiful
She's an angel
I tell you
She's incredible
I tell you
So gentle
So sweet
I love her so much
She's perfect
The mold was broken
After you

Princess in Paradise
3-7-95

You're my princess in paradise
So beautiful....So sensuous
You stand out from the rest
You definitely are the best
I am extremely impressed
With your beauty
Your kindness
You're my princess in paradise
So sensuous....So sweet
You can't be beat
Lacking in no manner
Excelling in everyway
And everyday
You're my princess in paradise
So sweet....So fine
Best of all
You're all mine

Perfect timing
8-13-09

I asked the universe
To send me an angel
She never came
I asked the universe
To send me a princess
She never came
I asked the universe
To send me a queen
She never came
Feeling discouraged
And a little sad
I asked the universe
Why haven't you answered my request?
Then the phone rang
I heard a soft comforting voice
I was so happy
The universe answered me
My angel, my princess, my queen
Had called me
I love her so much
Not only did the universe
Answer me
But gave me my best friend as well
Someone I can laugh with
Cry with
Be myself with
She does not judge me
Possesses ever quality I desire
The universe had a plan
And fulfilled it
At the perfect time

Beauty
3-5-94

Entranced by your love
I have fallen victim
To your Loveliness
Your beauty
Your inner strength
You are more beautiful than
The most colorful sunset
The most spectacular rainbow
Your beauty radiates brighter than the
Brightest star on the clearest night
Looking into your eyes
I know without a doubt
Without hesitation
You're the person I have
Been dreaming of
Dreaming of spending
The rest of my life with
Dreaming of loving more than
Than I have ever loved before
Dreaming of holding you
And never letting go
Your beauty is immeasurable
Immaculate
You are by far the
Absolute very best
And most dear person
I have ever and will ever meet
I love you more than the sky's above
I love you more than

Every planet and galaxy
In the universe put together
I love you more than anything
Anything
To see you sad
Makes me sad
So I just want to say
I love you
And I always will

She's My Everything
7-3-09

She's my every thing
Makes me happy
She's my world
Keeps me spinning
In the right direction
I would be so lost without her
Understanding in every way
She keeps me grounded
She keeps me calm
Relaxed
If I could give her the universe
And all of the glory
That comes with it
Would not be enough
To express my love for her
She's my every thing
Beautiful in everyway
She's an angel
Come to fill me with joy
Lucky I am to have met her
She's my every thing

My Past Time Love
12-7-89

She was pretty and smart
But we saw differently
I loved her from the start
A blink of the eye
And she was gone
Gone for ever
I loved her so much
Can't stop thinking of her
Wanting to be with her
Enough pain
I have to let her go
And move on
So painful
So painful
I love her so much
My past time love

Since I have Met You
2-13-92

Since I have met you
My life has changed
Every morning I wake
My absolute deepest and
Most wishful dream has come true
I have waited countless days
Weeks, months and years
To meet someone as beautiful
As you
Someone as special as you
With you by my side
I can accomplish anything
Overcome any obstacle
Build and climb any sky scraper
Make any dream come true
You are the best thing
That has happened to me
When you are away from me
My heart hurts
My body feels sick
You are my life

A Fun Time
2-10-90

Night life is for me
I feel so free
A beautiful person next to me
Someone smart to talk to
A picture was taken
Life is fun
So enjoyable
I feel your presence
A divine essence
I love your smile
Just think
I know the happiness
Life can bring
The joys to be found
They're all around
Have to find them
Lean on the higher source
I love to be
I want to be
I need to be
And free I am

Dreaming of you
10-6-87

Mysterious sweetheart
Out and waiting
Waiting for fun
Waiting for hope
Turning away
She'll be back someday
Trees sprout with life
Birds sing a heavenly tune
Wind blows softly
A full moon
A picture of a girl
I'm down but not asleep
I think of the color blue
I think of a way to be
Free from the heaviness
The pain
The everyday drain
Wanting so much more
Dreaming of you

Happy
2-22-94

I feel loved
I feel accepted
I feel happy
I feel wanted
I feel needed
I feel eccentric, energetic
An ebullience of your love
Has devoured my entire being
My love for you cannot be disclaimed
Disregarded nor disarrayed by apprehensiveness
My love for you is real
And cannot be measured
Nor abolished
My love for you
Does not bring disappointment
Rather an absolute abundance
Of bliss always and forever
You need not disbelieve
My willingness to die for you
I shall lay my life down
For you in order to save yours
My life means nothing
Without you
Without your love
Without your laughter
Without the everyday sound of your voice
Seeing your smile day after day
Fills me with divine exhilaration
Just your presence alone

Makes me want to divulge to you
You are extremely precious
To me
I love you more and more
Everyday
And remember my love for you
Will never ever die

Sensual Fragrance
11-9-92

I see you through an open window
So beautiful   so innocent
I can smell your sensual fragrance
Blowing past me in a cool breeze
Flowing through my window
I know I love you
I feel my need for you continuously growing
I want to hold your hand
You are so beautiful
I can see you staring at me
With your beautiful
Piquant brownish hazel eyes
Your smile melts me
I have to have you
All to myself
I want to spend my life with you
I want both of us
To share special memories together
I want to wake every morning
With you my side
You're the reason for existence
Live with me
Love me as I love you
Marry me
Hold me
Have children with me
My special one

Why
1-4-96

Looking into the sky
I always ask myself why?
What could there be
Beyond reality
Looking high above
I see a dove
And I ask myself
What would it be like?
To be so free
To fly so gracefully
In closing my eyes
I slipped into a dream
It seems
I remember seeing myself
Sitting on a bed of clouds
Overlooking several crowds
Crowds of people you see
And you know
They were all looking at me
So, I began to speak
Everything I was thinking
Was being transformed into adhesion
Among everyone
I remember feeling so much at peace
A feeling of being one with the universe
And the universe being one with me
What a feeling
Taking a deep breath
I awoke

Remembering my vision
Again, I looked into the sky
And ask myself why?
As the sky became illuminated
A feeling of peace
Consumed my entire being
Taking a deep breath
I put to rest
All of my anguish
All the pain
Animosity and anxiety
Seeing the dove again
Gracefully in flight
I whispered
Thank you my friend
For setting my mind free

My Special Love
5-21-09

I have a special love
I think of her everyday
I have a special love
She makes me happy
I have a special love
So kind and sweet
She deserves only the best
I have a special love
She turns me on
So sexy
So sexy
Lacking in no manner
I don't know who loves her more
Me, myself or I
I have a special love
She's perfect
I have always loved her
And always will
I have one dream
In life
To be happy
To feel calm
Relaxed
I want to feel
Myself with my perfect love
She's an angel
I once let her get away
She makes me real
She makes me a better person

I don’t want her to fly away again
She’s got it all
Funny, witty, clever
Smart
And a whole lot of fun
She’s perfect
Perfect in everyway

I Met a Girl

11-8-09

I've met a girl
I've met a girl
I've met a beautiful girl
She's incredible
She's delightful
Full of spirit
I've met a girl
I've met a girl
I've met a beautiful girl
I've known her for years
I've never met a girl
I can be myself with
Tell my deepest darkest secrets to
And no judgement will be made
She is the best
I love her so much
I've met a girl
I've met a girl
I've met a beautiful girl
Nice is life
Because of you
My stress is less
She brings me pleasure
She brings me clarity
She doesn't care to get in my head
And fill it full of egregious bullshit
She's full of life
She make things fun
I've met a girl
I've met a girl
I've met a beautiful girl

Life
2-16-84

As I walked into the room
I saw her pretty, shinning face
Staring into space
As I turned to leave the room
I hesitated, hoping to see her a second time
But when I turned around she was gone
For I know she was just an image
I had dreamed up in the back of my mind
Maybe there is such a person
But I know I will have to wait
Until the day of my end
Maybe she is waiting for me
Like the rest of my friends
I'll just have to wait and see
But it will be nice to know
If my dream I had thought
Up long ago came true
But as I always hear
Life is but a dream
And we must make the best of it
Even when life seems
To be falling apart
And pain and sorrow
Settles in
Keep on going until the end
But sometimes life can be good
And full of joy and happiness
And I guess that is just
God helping us get

Through the pain and depression
That has a tendency to hit us
When we least expect it
For I know that
Life has moments that are
Both happy and sad

With You by My Side
5-25-09

With you by my side
I can do anything
With you by side
I feel complete
You are by far
The very best
That has ever happened to me
You make me so happy
So excited
Feel so at peace
You are so beautiful
Inside and out
And in so many ways
You are an angel
You a princess
A queen
I am so honored and proud
To be with you
You're so beautiful
So exceptional in every way
And I must say
I am so happy to have you
In my life
With you by my side
I am complete

Soul Mate
10-4-03

Waking in the morning
Feeling kind of low
Feeling kind of blue
Until I met you
You make me feel appreciated
You make me feel wanted
You make me feel alive
You are so kind
And you're all mine
I love you with all my heart
All my soul
And I want you to know
I love you more than anyone alive
You're very dear to me
I think of the future
And all I see
Is just you and me
Forever
My love for you is very deep
I will never stop loving you
Never stop caring for you
You're my life
Because of you
I love life
And everything life has to offer
You are very smart
And very beautiful
You have lots of ambition
Lots of hope and dreams

I am very proud of you
Proud of all your accomplishments
You are very special
And very gifted
You offer a lot
You are an angel
You are my life
And I will never stop loving you.

I See Her Beauty
12-22-09

I see her beauty
In the sky
So, vast
So, full of energy
I see her beauty
In the ocean
So, massive
The strength
The beauty
The power
Everlasting tranquility
I see her beauty
In everyday life
No matter how I feel
Whether I'm angry, depressed
Sick or down and out
The beauty is
I know she is
Thinking of me
As I am thinking
Of her
And I know
She loves me
As much as I
Love her
She is my angel
She is my life
I see her beauty
In the stars

The galaxies
The universe
I see her beauty
In everything

My Angel

4-28-02

I met my Angel today
And I let her get away
I met my Angel today
And I let her get away
She made me feel happy
She made me feel glad
She made me feel lucky
And I let her get away
I met my angel today
And I let her get away
I met my angel today
And I let her get away
I saw her from a distance
And she drew me in
With her mysterious ambiance
There was something about her
The way she moved
The way she talked
She was so pretty
And she glowed
I met my angel today
And I let her get away
I met my angel today
And I let her get away
She was all mine
She was kind
She had it all
And I loved everything about her
I met my angel today
And I let her get away

Ups And Downs
2-5-96

We've had our ups
We've had our downs
Our highs and our lows
Thank you for starting over
Giving me another try
While we were apart
I'd dream of you often
I'd think of you everyday
Praying and praying
This day has finally come
Because I knew
With you by my side
We can accomplish it all
I am glad we decided to work together
I do promise to do whatever it takes
To make you happy
I will go the extra mile
Not just for a short while
But forever because you are very special to me
And I love you too much
To lose you again

My Special One
11-09-92

I see you through an open window
So, innocent.... So, sweet
I can smell your sensual fragrance
Blowing past me in a cool breeze
Flowing through my open window
I know I love you
I feel my need for you
Continuously growing
You are so beautiful
I can see you staring at me
With your beautiful brownish eyes
Your smile melts me
You must be mine
All to myself
I want to spend my life with you
I want to wake up every morning
With you by my side
You're the reason for my existence
Live with me
Love me as I love you
My special one

Happiness
12-11-91

I can see your smile
For a mile
Your hair blowing widely free
In the wind
Your beautiful brown eyes
Have a very piquant sparkle to them
Holding you puts me in bliss
I am so happy to have met you
You are everything to me
I am always thinking of you
Dreaming of you
Wanting to be with you
In times of pain and depression
Or happiness
I am always here for you
Your effusive ways
Are very comforting to me
And I am happy
To be a part of your life

Desire
4-15-02

You are very piquant
I find your demeanor
To be nothing less than effusive
When I'm in your elegant
Presence, I am succumbed
By your beauty of everything
You are
I have an impetus desire
To be with you
You are a rainbow
In the mist
Sunshine on a cloudy day
A single flower in
A dry lake bed
The beauty that encapsulates
An entire city
And best of all
You are all mine.

Dreams
5-14-87

Dreams to find
Dreams to dream
I wake to a mystery
Finding the way
Standing tall
Getting hit with obstacles
Again and again
Down on a knee
Giving up is not an option
I miss her so much
The pain won't leave
Won't go away
Dreams to find
Dreams to dream
Dreaming of her
She's in my head
All the time
Can't sleep
Can't function
I love her
And I can't stop dreaming of her

Moonlight Sensation

9-7-87

A full moon
A cool moon
Feeling the vibes
Love is in the air
Blanketing your being
A beautiful woman
Sensual irresistibility
A warm breeze
Sand at your feet
The smell of the ocean
Waves crackle
The moonlight blanketing
Everything with the brilliance of
All that is
All that can be
My beautiful love
I love you so much
Holding her tightly
Feeling her tenderness
Her love
My moonlight Sensation

Blissful
4-20-09

When I wake
I get excited because I know
Where ever I go
And whatever I do
Whatever song I choose to sing
And whatever thought I choose to ponder on
Someone special is thinking of me
A friend close to my heart
A comrade for life
She puts a smile on my face
And a tickle in my fancy
She's, beautiful on the inside
As well as the outside
And I know
Whatever problem I face
Whatever situation I'm in
Whether good or bad
Someone special is thinking of me
And whatever face I look into
I think of you
And whatever eyes
I stare into
They're not
As beautiful as yours
You are eccentric
And exquisite
Exotic
As well as euphoric
Your beauty is mesmerizing

Enhancing and embracing
Seductive yet tender
And I know
Whatever psychological mountain
I am forced to climb
And whatever decision I choose to make
Whether good or bad
Understandable or confusing
It doesn't matter
Because I know
My special friend
Is thinking of me

2
INSENSITIVE INVOLVEMENT

Feelings Within
9-23-91

We all have needs. We all have wants
We all have expectations
Extreme duration
We all have dreams. We all have feelings
We all have pressures
We all feel pain. We all want to refrain
Refrain from malaise
The feeling of absolute discomfort
Absolute agitation
We all feel love. We all feel warmth
A comfortable feeling, a sense of healing
We all wonder. We all blunder
We all have emotions-notions
Often we all feel like
Deviating from existence
Departing for awhile
We all have nightmares
We all have uplifting thoughts
Best of all
We all have each other and
We need to love one another

Emotional Pain
5-23-96

Sitting on stain pine
I can hear you whine
All you do is complain
Greed has infested your mind
You're no longer kind
And you're blind to see
You're losing me
I love you so much
More and more everyday
But I can't continue to hurt this way
The emotional pain is too much
I know you're confused
I know you've been hurt
However, I do know
If you give me your self again
We can begin
To repair the broken pieces
That hurt us in the past
And our marriage will last and last
You know I love you
You know I want you
But, I don't need you
You know my feelings for you
Are far too great to give up
I don't know what to do any more
I feel I'm losing you
And we're drifting apart
More and more everyday
But don't ever forget
I really do love you

Enough
8-20-09

I've had enough
I dreamt of being with a girl
Like you
And then I woke up
Next to you
And found you are cruel
Mean spirited and bad tempered
I've had enough
You rant and rave
I find you depraved
A screw lose
In your brain
Always causing pain
I've had enough
I loved you dearly
And clearly we are a wrong fit
You constantly scream and yell
What the hell
Sporadic brain impairment
Impulsive and explosive in nature
I've had enough

Done
11-9-06

I am done
Screen me out
I am done
You did me wrong
Bent the truth
Screen me out
I am done
I don't care anymore
I gave you everything
Everything I am
Everything I had to offer
You are foul
You are sour
You are a coward
I am done
Scrofulous intent
Screen me out
I don't care anymore

I can't Take It
9-17-97

My friend went insane
Something snapped
In his brain
Pumped full of drugs
Got to shut him down
Pumped full of drugs
Got to shut him down
Because without them
He acts like a clown
Dangerous at times
Got to shut him down
Complication becoming his reality
Confusion becoming his comfort
Broken and frail
Broken and frail
Hail to the chief
Wandering fields of imaginary concepts
Let's take a ride
Try it on his side
Guaranteed to be outrageous
Operating just short of being conscious
Manipulation breaking him down
"I can't take it!"
"I can't take it!"
Feeling the pressure
Comatosed by his own subconscious
"I can't take it!"
"I can't take it!"
He squeals

His skin becoming blistered
With feelings of betrayal
Dancing with the laughter
Of insanity
In the name of uncertainty
"I can't take it!"
"I can't take it!"
Again he proclaims
Pumped full of drugs
Got to shut him down

3

WONDERING IN THE FIELDS OF REALITY

Preconceived Notions
9-22-13

Expectations caused by centrifugal
Explosions of assimilated
Complexity, materialized by
An infusion of intricate
Grid like patterns
Subconsciously imprinted
Over long periods of time
Causing your mind
To think and act
According to preconceived notions
Materialized by an
Atmospheric indulgence
Of a consumed absorption
Of previous executions

Super Charge
8-22-96

Insignificant interpretations of
Infallible intricate articulation
He was walking along the beach
When it happened
As he gazed into the sunset
A feeling of animation
Consumed him
Becoming one with the universe
Up from the seam of society
Stretching beyond infinity
Destiny at its finest
"Freedom", He shouts
"I must have freedom!"
Excitement
Electrifying impulses
Super charge
Dominated by brilliance
Succumbed at the hand of
A subconscious manipulation
Of bureaucratic involvement
"Enough!", He shouts…….. "Enough!"

Impairment
7-21-96

Focusing on disillusioned ideas
Laughing at controversial impairment
Living according to egregious encroachment
No validity what so ever
A parasite internally intertwined
Among all of us
An outrageous idea of mine
We all have it
Spoken different
Received one way
Projected another
The beauty of life
Diversity constantly occurring
Interspersion a must
Especially amongst all of us

Mathematical Intuition
3-10-98

Mathematical intuition
Is not for me
Circumcised from the left
Left is definitely
Not the best
But right is very bright
In a hemispheric sense
Condensation of left over pieces
Of the past
Can't quite rid the gray
The fucking dismay
Of a foul time
Stress revolutionizing into dictatorship
Causing bitterness and heartburn
And my blood boils
Broken promises
Becoming the acceptance
You break your word
I consider you a turd
An ass I may be
At least I'm me

Blistered

Assumed accomplishment
Blistered with feelings of bitterness
Caused by an ignorant regurgitation
Of callous and impetuous subconscious
Imprinted embedment of thought
Saturated by the most compromised
And ill-fated debauchery
An over whelming of the mind
The being
The human
The control of it all
An ongoing infusion of hypocrisy
A pervious sponge like manipulation
Causing an internal struggle
Between right and wrong

Warmth
10-03-96

Only a creative mind
Can untwine
A tangled expression
Misery and pain
Drains a brain
However, Laughter
Comforts the mind
A security blanket for a short while
Trying to forget the journey I took
Walking through the unforgiving
Fields of abandonment
Abundant in size
A hidden prize
Lies just beneath the surface
A window into the souls of many
Clever and wise
Though I am
I missed my prize
Due to its monolith disguise
Felling trapped in complication
I turn to see
What's become of me
Plagued by contaminated thought
I see nothing
I feel nothing
Held back by my own ignorance
Each foot step I take
Begins to evaporate
Myself being into nowhere

With very little left
I know I must give my best
With a hedonistic leap
I have put to shame
The unruly fields
I have once walked

Lost
9-99-92

Trapped in the past
No-where to go
Shielded by existence
And I want to run
Run.... Run.... Run
I want to
Run.... Run.... Ron
Disillusioned by introverted
Articulated concepts of anticipation
Frustrated by not knowing
How can one relay or present a message
If the idea is not to be thought of
Lingering in the fields of lost dreams
Lost hope
Lost fantasies
Lost ideas
Falling.... Falling
Faster and faster into no where
Trapped with no way out
I'm lost never to be found again
Good bye!

Dark Ride

Darkness descends upon the town
City blanketed by constitutional
Irrelevance
Appetite motivated by chronic
Delusions of apathy
Disregard for the dark mist
The dark ride
Holding on to pride
Children cry
People die
I sigh
And life continues
Diabolical disengagement of
Dismembered psychological embarrassment
An expansion of carbohydrates
Infusion of catalytic emptiness
Swimming in the tangled
Rip-tides of expansion
Blanketing myself with the warmth
Of a universal assimilated
Thought process called humanity

Expansion
8-14-91

The correlation of two minds
Intertwining together
Coming up with a distinctly correct hypothesis
May be impressive.... However
An extreme introvert
Reluctant to share
A part of him or herself
Caused by an overpowering
Abusive childhood
Carrying on into the future of this persons
Subconscious fetal mind
Causing severe depression and maliciousness
Converting into violence
Suddenly engaged by an intense self-realism
And change of thinking habits
By such a person
Systematically,
Causing a total reproduction of the mind
Converting the person into an extrovert
In his or her adult life
Now that's impressive!

Confused
4-6-00

Ignorance manipulated by insecurity
A manifest of self-absorbed criticism
Plagued by uncertainty
Evolving into
Psychological subconscious paranoia
Stricken by a personality disorder
Happy and sad
Joyful and distraught
An introvert by nature
Dangerously indecisive
An egregious displacement
Of emotions
Psychological impairment
A chemical imbalance
Notoriously confused
Smothered by a saturation of
Subconscious hallucinations
Vanity prevails
Always

Humble and wise
7-21-96

Humble and wise is the lonely man
Always thinking
Sometimes drinking
But always thinking
No one to really turn to
Because he's on his own
Everyone's back at home
Several thousand miles away
So, he begins to pray
Taking it day by day
Holding on to hope
He refuses to give up
On and on he goes
A certain inner obsession
Breaking through the depression
Disenchanted by skepticism
Turned off by criticism
He's determined to make it
Though tired of coming home to loneliness
On and on he goes
Again, he begins to think
Shedding a tear
He drinks another beer
Relying on inner strength
Moving at a descent pace
"Things will get better!"
He convinces himself
"I know it's true!"

Tough times
Down to dimes
So watch out
Because here I come

Isolation
8-17-96

Dark desolate isolation
A feeling of egregious contemptuousness
Wandering in fields
Of vacuous oblivion
Finding comfort in
Obstinateness and obstreperousness
Be yourself
Do not conform
May be difficult
May want to give in
Be unique
Set the example
Happy to see
No one like me
Words of inspiration
Be a leader
Lead the flock

Gray day

I take a face of ignorance
I walk a line of assertiveness
Overcoming these obstacles set before me
Dreary and gray at times
Impatients is vast today
My shadow
Playing tricks on me
Confused by the many paths to take
Some make you
Some make you.... Fake
Some complicated
Some obsolete
Some you cannot touch
No matter how much you try
The world is mine
Often taken away
Starting over again and again
The selfishness of a precocious world
Suffer in-order to succeed
Laziness will assure nothing
Walking the fine line of insanity
Laughing out-loud
Feeling the pain
Of a fallen reign
Criticized for being energized
Society has become
Fallen and fake
Experienced by many
The terrible shame
Of society and their game

Mindful Manipulation
4-21-17

Archeological brilliance devastated
By a mindful manipulation
Of illogical importance
An egregious encroachment
Of Hedonism
Self-deprecated involvement
Constricted entanglement of
Strangulated character
Developed by an accumulation
Of involuntary subconscious
Existence
An evolution of dictated
Over analyzed thought
Image controlled by a vacuous
Portal of lost interpreted
Conceived imagery of painted
Speculated watered down
Appendages controlled by
Aimless wandering
Sour stench of lost self
Buried by confused behavior

Regurgitated Isolation
4-14-17

Living in an ocean of
Regurgitated isolation
Subconscious embarrassment
A Past time replicated
Sandwich made with generous portions
Of guilt marinated in a sauté of arrogance
Followed by a dark shadow
Materializing into reality
Feeding off-of internal misery
Wrapping yourself in a warm blanket
Plagued with a saturation of anticipated
Self-worth
Living according to prosperous
Inflammatory speculated
Adverse self-absorbed confusion
Value manipulated by a pervious
Misevaluated experience
Consuming the internal identity
Of complete self
False image
A lifetime scrimmage

Bastardized Brilliance
1-7-17

Superfluous infiltration of a subconscious
Conceptual reenactment of imaginary compliance
Saturated by overwhelming and overbearing
Thoughts of desire and acceptance
A psychological and sociological picnic
Manifested realism of bastardized brilliance
Proclaimed visions of a justified existence
Allocated sensationalism of self
Criticized behavior caused by internal
Visions of accomplishment
Introverted finite explosive remembrance
Of an insoluble sinkhole of indecisiveness

Saturated Superfluous Inferiority

12-7-16 (Co-written by my brother Eric)

Discombobulated triage of emotions
Smothered by a strangulation
Of confused bureaucratic influence
A sycophant entangled in a diametric
Compulsion of inconsistent awareness
Saturated superfluous inferiority
Manifested by an ardent complication
Of an overwhelming desire, to
Mollycoddle in a fabricated understanding
Of one's animistic nature
An ethereal cloud cover
Butchered narcissism
Materializing into buried
Repressed arrogance
Only to find a vapid
Awareness of reality
Living a vacuous existence
A mind soaked with skepticism
Pickled with ignorance
I have only one thing to say
How disconsolate

Incineration of Self
12-9-16

Evaporated telepathic insecurity
A hologram of spontaneous virtue
Exacerbated feelings of reality
Unconscious liberation
A culmination of self- evaluated
Importance
An incineration of self
Bombastic calculations of
Therapeutic ridicule
Proportionate scurrilous pervious
Sponge like absorption
Callused ego
Blistered with eccentric vibrations
A blended sunrise
Intertwined with hypocrisy
Bureaucratic manipulated arrogance
Manifested coagulations of
Repercussions
Blistered confusion
A mirage of hyperextended circulatory
Inconvenience

Aware
10-31-16

Seasonal recklessness
Estranged entanglement
Artificial discombobulated theory
Immense evaporated culture
Slurries of anticipated realistic reasoning
Manifested hedonism
Self-propagated relevance
Of saturated benevolence
Blind Apparitions
Clouded fear strangled by insomnia
Ethereal existence
Blanketed by conscious speculated awareness
Cosmic enterprise
Entrepreneurial explications
Overwhelming concertation
Peeled narcissism
Divulgence of implicated thought
Smothered fragrance of
Exuberant materialistic certainty

Monolithic Value
10-11-16

Cataclysmically twisted evolution
An expansion of self- mutilated thought
A divulgence of materialistic insomnia
Complexity and depth intertwined with
Aspirations of development
Impartial reality
Apprehensive diversity
Ending in squander
Blanketed by the warmth
Of sophisticated irony
Plagued by confusion and indecisiveness
Of the systematical relations
Between tarnished bravery
And Karmic implications
Severed contrast
Bastardized by judgement
Elongated recapitulated accountability
Visions of a diplomatic fusion
Of brilliance
The sweet aroma of
Emancipated self

Malicious Understanding
1-26-17

Scurrilous escalation derived by
A malicious understanding of a
Subconscious Imprinted education
Of a fallacy nature
Miscalculated deception by
A subconscious absorption
Of individual callousness
Allocated sycophant motivated by
An exercised movement of
Insensitive and insecure
Ignorance of reality
Bilateral calibrated celebration of
Evolutionary excuses
Entitled development caused by
An over- zealous community
Manipulated by an extrication
Of internal turmoil
Feverish alimony
Discovered internal destruction of
A fire ball of disillusioned thought
Warped aborted under estimated
Brilliant understanding of misguided
Interpretation of cohesive creativity
An injection of pastime conformity

Vacuous In Nature

5-9-17

Recycled regurgitated simplistic thought
Counterbalanced by arrogance
Vacuous in nature
Transparent in design
Sponge like absorption
Of a lifetime of confusion
Miscalculated interpretation of experience
Buried by conflicting and reoccurring
Visions of hopefulness
Empathy followed by capitalism
Scarred by truth
Evolutionary involvement
Revolutionary counterproductive impersonation
Of self
Blistered mind
Lifetime blind
Imagery and visionary
Materializing into a warped
Atmospheric comfort
Communal displacement of
Educated squander

Atmospheric Involvement

1-15-17

Exposed mirage of a Neanderthal exquisite
Contemporary vessel powered by desperation
Realism destroyed by an ambush of buried
Imprinted relaxation of melted evolution
Blistered confusion
Analytical diverse accomplishment
Failure derived by scurrilous embarrassment
Manifested calculations of useless empathy
Specialized elusive complex insomnia
Energized delusions of materialized application
Blanket warmth of irony
Driven by miscalculated self-characterized
Euphoric sensational capitalization of
Schizophrenic involvement
Thoughts interfered by thought
Empowered blasphemy
Manipulated existence broken by
Expectations
Conscious breath
Exhausted introverted turmoil of
Shattered wealth

Solicitation
12-28-16

Overwhelming counter productive
Solicitation of a cauterization
Of self
A molten circulation
Incineration of all that is
Materialized absorption of disappointment
Caused by a self- subjection to fallacy
Intricate persona imbalance
Driven by malice incompetence
Vindictive involvement
Callous integrity
Blasphemous evolution
Stabilization of impression
An overcompensation of value
Disassociated overwhelming embarrassment
Contradictory allocated visions of promise
A sanctuary of sorts
False brilliance
Evaporated self
Tangled evaluation
A strangulation of involvement

Vehement Displacement
12-10-17

Mamas going crazy
Visions of insanity
Images of complexity
Delusional aspirations
Mamas got a little helper
She needs some help
Lost in a vortex of confusion
Madness cries out
In an endless cry for sorrow
A cry for help
Smiles aren't real
Chained by indifference
Callas nature
Blistered confrontation
Mamas going crazy
Consumed by the
Digestion of a brilliant color
Perceived in a past time existence
Encapsulated by brilliance
Only she can understand
Delivered nonsense of
Extricated involvement
Brave intention
Sarcastic evaporation
Misunderstood exacerbated conscious
A collage of emptiness
Blistered thoughts of
Regurgitated self
Mamas needs help
Because mamas going crazy

Selfish and Lazy
11-13-10

Society has become
So, corrupt
So, selfish
So, ungrateful
Obsessed with self- inflicted insecurity
Inflated self-image
Self-respect
Self-esteem
Worried about others opinion
Causing a life of
Subconscious manipulated corruption
Because of ignorance
Due to an individual
Selfish laziness
Easier to find fault in others
Look inside and rid the mold
The mildew
The rust
Of past time dust
Left behind
Flush the core
Then you can know
What you are for

Lost souls
12-31-03

Sing to the lost souls of evolution
The revolutionary anticipation of
Dreary disregard
High and low
Sing to the lost souls of insanity
A sanctuary of mental interlude
Compilation of distorted rubbish
Do you see the rainbow?
Magical and mysterious
Sing to the lost souls
Of the serpent
Jaws of perception
Carnivorous in nature
Swallowing you whole
Feel its power
Slithering and sweet
Sing to the lost souls of the universe
Drink from the earth
Cry the tears of jubilation
Water drops of change
And phallus leaves its mark

Death
5-26-13
(Co-written by my Daughter Amber)

Saddened by demise
Hearing all the cries
Cutting many ties
Every time someone dies
My life is forced to change
Everything has been rearranged
Life has become strange
I feel like I'm wondering on the range
Turning another page
Feeling trapped in a cage
Feeling rage
Wanting to burn some sage
Trying to cleanse my soul
At times, feels like a shattered bowl
Sometimes taking its toll
Feeling less than whole
Wanting to run
Wanting to cry
Feeling scared
Feeling alone
Life can hard
Life can be unfair
My heart has a tear
What a bare
A bare I burden
A pain I endure
The pain is so pure
Is there no cure

Saddened by the cycle of life
Stricken with strife
Feeling like I've been
Stabbed by a knife
Is there no hope
Why do I keep hearing the word nope?
As hard as life may be
Love I can always see

Catalytic Emptiness
10-15-16

Diabolical disengagement of
Dismembered psychological embarrassment
An expansion of carbohydrates
Infusion of catalytic emptiness
Swimming in the tangled
Rip tides of expansion
Blanketing my self
With the warmth
Of a universal assimilated
Thought process
Called humanity

Mind
5-19-88

I sit here watching television
I hear the phone ring
Wondering why
I begin to sigh
Who could it be?
Why do I scare?
Who's out there?
I can't help but think
It's my shrink
My minds okay
So go away
I've been in and out
Now I shout
The hell with this
Breaking away
I found the way
But I keep in mind
Who's to fame?
Who's to shame?
Who's to blame?
Why this game?
I was sitting on the edge of a star
Overlooking man's own madness
I took a leap and splashed into realism
Up from the seam of society
Stretching over the laughter of insanity
Out of my hand I once saw realism
Now I see plastic

Thought
6-3-13

Atmospheric interludes of relevance
Regarding past time existences
Governed by thought
Brought on by cohesive existence
Of opinions of others
Assimilation a must
Calibrating your being
Forever seeing the truth
Of an evolutionary fulfillment
Of happiness
Projection of self
A manipulation of force
A human stance
A powerful stance
A graceful prance
Love and light
So bright
So sincere
So pure
Angelic enlightenment
Beautiful and magical
Ever so encapsulating
An extrication of purity
And dexterity
Ethereal brilliance
Captured by an evaporation
Of human knowledge
Allow, except and let be
The universe has spoken

Chance and expectation
Has been broken
Thought is limiting
If there is a negative infiltration
A human world torn
Between right and wrong

Idealistic Identification
11-13-16

Bombastic urination of
The ultimate clearance
In a systematic validation
Of a feverish fabrication
Of idealistic identification
Brought on by the moralization
Of Societal implosion and
Irreprehensible existence
Justified by an intoxicated
State of exuberated and
Exhilarated introversion of self
Manipulated with care

A Tribute to Jim
5-15-84

Waking to a shower of indescribable colors
And they're in my mind
At first I panic
Then I wonder where they came from
I got out of bed
And came to a hall
It was warm and dark
Smelt of green happiness
Voices laughing distantly
Feeling like I'm being watched
So I walked on down the hall
Came to a light
Walking into the light
I became a different form
Out here
We are joyful
Eccentric and magnificent
I turned to leave
But something became of me
Forget the night
You have made it
To the ultimate enlightenment

INDEX OF FIRST LINES

A special thank you to my good friend Al Mata,
your help on this book was greatly appreciated.
A humble thank you again my friend.

Synoptical Firing of Electrical Complexity is a compilation of poems written over several years, mainly focusing on love, anxiety and analytical psychology.

I have always been fascinated with nature and life itself. Over the years I have wanted more than ever to understand how everything works. As a child growing up, I was always curious as to why people act and say what they do. I believe we are all curious beings and curiosity is a blessing.

Unfortunately too many of us tend to follow rather than lead; thus being so hurtful at times just for acceptance by the masses, or sheep as I call them (Individuals who can't think for themselves and believe everything they hear from the majority). These same people, away from crowds, can be some of the most loving, friendly and generous people. WHY?

Why change who you are to appease others? I have known many people like this over the years, and the sad part is every one of these people lost all their friends. No one cares to be around them because of the toxic energy they dispense. There is absolutely no inner peace with these individuals.

I wanted more than ever to understand this behavioral imbalance. Moreover, I wanted to help everyone become better people, happier people, ridding all the misery often caused by an unbalance of the mind and soul. I have made it my life long journey to help everyone become balanced. We all have the ability to become enlightened. Most often, all we need is some direction.

I hope these poems help individuals become more loving and grateful. Most of all, I hope to teach individuals how to continue being themselves and not falling into the subconscious sinkhole of an absorbed pickling of contaminated thought.

Peace always my friends.

Transformed phosphorus

Transaction of educated

Previous notions belittled

By existence inhabiting

An intermission of disguised

Acclimated appearance of

A cauterization of nonsense

Don't follow the masses

BE YOURSELF

www.ingramcontent.com/pod-product-compliance
Lightning Source LLC
LaVergne TN
LVHW051955060526
838201LV00059B/3658
* 9 7 8 1 4 7 8 7 9 7 6 7 8 *